THE RESCUE
PLAN

THE PATH OF GRACE FROM
SIN TO SALVATION

Priscilla Coker-Durotola

ISBN:
979-828-983-534-5

Designed and Published by:
The Book Surgeons International
+2347061082014
Email: thebooksurgeons@gmail.com

**To connect with the author,
you can reach out to her via**

Instagram: @thegirllovedbygod
@priscillaevangelicalministry
@booksbypriscilla.co
Email: cokerpriscilla@gnail.com

iii

Table Of Content

Dedication

Within this fragile frame, a treasure divine
Not mine to boast, but His to shine.
So when strength breaks through my weakness,
It's His glory, not my greatness.
2 Corinthians 4:7

I dedicate this book to God who loved me and qualified me through Jesus Christ to herald His Glory.

Acknowledgement

To my dad, (Baba Coker as I fondly call him), my mentor and fellow author, I am a lot like you than I thought. Thank you for living an exemplary life of godliness, humility and submission.

To my husband, PMD, you have helped me witness the transformative power of the gospel of Christ simply by observing you. You are a good man my love.

To my mum, Mama Coker and sister, Funto Okubena, God placed you in my life to constantly show me what I am capable of doing. I am forever grateful for your constant encouragement. I am so blessed.

To my beautiful daughters, Sophia and Irene - my gifts from God, I pray the content of this book is simple enough for you to understand what God has done for you in Christ Jesus and it helps you see how important you are in God's plan.

To Pastor Ire Ogunsina, thank you for faithfully honouring the gospel and wholeheartedly delivering it just as you have received it. Under your leadership, my spiritual growth has been both steady and significant.

To the rescued, many are still lost. Let us align with the mission and extend the hope we've received.

To the lost, you are not forgotten. There is a living rescue plan already in motion for you.

Jesus Christ be glorified forever! It's all you Lord.

Introduction

What is the Gospel?

> *Moreover, brethren, I declare to you the gospel which I preached to you, which also you received and in which you stand, by which also you are saved, if you hold fast that word which I preached to you—unless you believed in vain.*
>
> *For I delivered to you first of all that which I also received: that Christ died for our sins according to the Scriptures, and that He was buried, and that He rose again the third day according to the Scriptures.*
>
> *—1 Corinthians 15:1 - 4 NKJV*

We often hear the word "gospel." We may have even used it ourselves or heard it referenced in sermons, songs, or conversations. For some, it's just another

Christian term used mainly to identify with the faith. For others, it simply means "good news." But what is this good news really about? And why is it good?

To grasp the depth and power of the word "gospel," we must first understand its historical and cultural context. The word we now associate with salvation and Christian faith had royal, political, and prophetic roots. In the first-century Roman Empire, the Greek term *euangelion*, translated as "gospel" or "good news," was used to announce significant public events such as the rise of a new emperor or a military victory. These announcements declared peace, salvation, and order ushered in by Caesar, who was often hailed as a "saviour."

One historical example is the Priene Inscription (9 BC), which describes the birthday of Caesar Augustus as "the beginning of the good news (*euangelion*) for the world." The emperor was presented as a divine figure whose reign brought peace and salvation to the known world. A section of the inscription reads:

"Providence... has set in the most perfect order by giving us Augustus... sending him as a saviour... that he might end war and arrange all things... and since

the birthday of the god Augustus was the beginning of the good tidings (euangelion) for the world..."

In this context, when the early Christians proclaimed "the gospel of Jesus Christ," they weren't simply sharing a spiritual message—they were making a radical and dangerous claim: that Jesus, not Caesar, is Lord. This was more than religious language; it was a bold declaration of a new King, a true Saviour, and a greater Kingdom.

Mark opens his Gospel with:

> *"The beginning of the gospel of Jesus Christ, the Son of God."* (Mark 1:1)

Before the Roman world embraced the term, the Hebrew Scriptures already spoke of "good news." In the Old Testament, the phrase often pointed to God's reign, salvation, and restoration:

> - *"How beautiful on the mountains are the feet of those who bring good news... who proclaim salvation, who say to Zion, 'Your God reigns!'"* —Isaiah 52:7

> • *"The Spirit of the Sovereign Lord is on me... to proclaim good news to the poor..."* —Isaiah 61:1

The Jewish people longed for this promised Saviour—the Messiah—who would fulfil these prophecies. Jesus boldly declared that He was that fulfilment:

> *"Today this Scripture is fulfilled in your hearing."* —Luke 4:18-21

Jesus and His apostles gave the gospel its eternal meaning. It was no longer tied to an earthly ruler or a temporal victory; it was the divine declaration of God's eternal triumph over sin and death through Christ. The gospel tells the greatest story ever told:

- Jesus lived a sinless life.
- He died for the sins of the world.
- He rose from the grave.
- And He now reigns as King over all creation.

> *"Jesus went into Galilee, proclaiming the good news of God. 'The time has come,' he said. 'The kingdom of God has come near. Repent and believe the good news!'"*
> —Mark 1:14-15.

In a time when Caesar claimed peace through conquest, Jesus brought peace through the cross. In a world ruled by empires, He ushered in the Kingdom of God. In a society driven by power and pride, He came in humility and sacrifice.

At its heart, the gospel is the good news of Jesus Christ—and it truly is good, joyful, liberating, life-giving news. It proclaims forgiveness of sins, reconciliation with God, and the gift of eternal life through the atoning work of Christ. It is God's plan of redemption—restoring a broken humanity to Himself in love, justice, and grace.

To fully understand the depth of the gospel, we must first understand the key characters who shape the story. Each of the following chapters will explore one of these central figures or themes:

- God, the loving Creator, whose plan has never changed.

- Satan, the deceiver, exposed.

- Man, the fallen image-bearer, is still deeply pursued.

- Jesus, the perfect, divine Rescuer.

- The Holy Spirit, our seal, our strength, our guide.

- The Bible, the trustworthy, living roadmap of God's truth.

Understanding these characters gives us clarity—not just about what the gospel is, but about why it matters, what it offers, and how it invites us to respond.

CHAPTER

GOD—THE LOVING CREATOR WHOSE PLAN HAS NEVER CHANGED

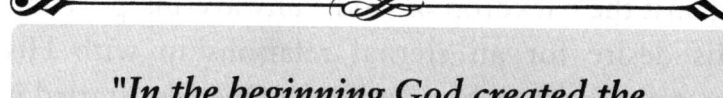

"In the beginning God created the heavens and the earth."
— Genesis 1:1

B efore we can appreciate the depth of the gospel message, we must begin where the story begins: with God. He is not a distant force or an indifferent deity. He is the loving Creator who created the universe with intentionality, beauty, and purpose. Understanding who God is—His nature, His heart, and His original design for humanity—is foundational to understanding the gospel.

The good news is only truly good when we see it against the backdrop of God's unwavering plan and His desire for an eternal relationship with His creation. So let us begin with the One who started it all: the Author of life, the Ruler of all, and the Father whose love never fails.

To comprehend God in His fullness is beyond human ability.

As **Job 11:7–9** reflects:

> *"Can you fathom the mysteries of God? Can you probe the limits of the Almighty? They are higher than the heavens above—what can you do? They are deeper than the depths below—what can you know? Their measure is longer than the earth and wider than the sea."*

God is infinite, eternal, and unsearchable in many ways. Yet He is not unknowable.

Throughout Scripture, He has revealed Himself clearly and consistently, beginning from the very first chapter of Genesis.

In Genesis, God is introduced as the Creator of all things:

> *"In the beginning, God created the heavens and the earth."*
> — Genesis 1:1.

This declaration sets the foundation for understanding God as sovereign and supreme—One who brings order, beauty, and life out of nothing. His creative power is unmatched. With a word, light was brought out of darkness:

> *"And God said, 'Let there be light,' and there was light."*
> — Genesis 1:3.

This divine speech alone speaks volumes of God's authority and omnipotence.

God is also purposeful and intentional. Creation was no accident; it followed an orderly design, culminating in the creation of humanity:

> *"So God created mankind in His own image, in the image of God He created them; male and female He created them."*
> — Genesis 1:27.

This act reveals not only divine craftsmanship but God's intent to allow humanity to reflect His nature, steward His creation, and live in relationship with Him.

Unlike distant deities of pagan belief systems, the God of the Bible is relational and personal. He walked with

Adam and Eve in the garden, demonstrating His desire for closeness and communion:

> *"Then the man and his wife heard the sound of the Lord God as He was walking in the garden..."*
> **— Genesis 3:8.**

This intimate fellowship was central to His design for creation. God didn't just make humanity— He made us to know Him, and to be known by Him.

Yet God is also holy and just. When Adam and Eve disobeyed, God responded with righteous judgment:

> *"Cursed is the ground because of you... for dust you are and to dust you will return."*
> **— Genesis 3:17, 19.**

Holiness demands accountability. Still, amid judgment, we see a God full of mercy. He clothed Adam and Eve, covering their shame:

> *"The Lord God made garments of skin for Adam and his wife and clothed them."*
> **— Genesis 3:21.**

Even more importantly, He gave a prophetic promise of redemption:

> *"He will crush your head, and you will strike His heel."*
> — Genesis 3:15.

This verse is widely recognised as the first messianic prophecy, pointing to Christ's ultimate victory over Satan.

Throughout the unfolding story of humanity, God remained faithful. He is a covenant-keeping God, establishing lasting promises with Noah, Abraham, Isaac, and Jacob.

> • **To Noah***: "I will establish my covenant with you."* —Genesis 9:9.

> • **To Abraham:** *"All peoples on earth will be blessed through you."* —Genesis 12:3.

These covenants were not just historical agreements. They were divine assurances that God's redemptive plan would not be thwarted by human failure.

Central to God's nature is love. This love is not passive or abstract—it is active, sacrificial, and transformational:

> *"For God so loved the world that He gave His only Son..."*
> — John 3:16.

Paul affirms this as well:

> *"But God demonstrates His love for us in this: while we were still sinners, Christ died for us"*
> (Romans 5:8).

The apostle John echoes:

> *"God is love... Whoever lives in love lives in God, and God in them"*
> (1 John 4:16).

And again:

> *"Whoever does not love does not know God, because God is love"*
> (1 John 4:8).

This divine love is also described in the Old Testament:

> *"I have loved you with an everlasting love; I have drawn you with lovingkindness"* (Jeremiah 31:3).

Unlike human affection, God's love is unchanging, everlasting, and undeserved. It is the foundation of our relationship with Him and the motivation behind His redemptive plan. The nature of God is also spiritual.

> *"God is spirit, and His worshipers must worship in the Spirit and in truth."*
> —John 4:24.

This means that God is not confined by space or time. He is omnipresent, everywhere at once; He is eternal, having neither beginning nor end. Paul exalts this truth beautifully:

> *"To the King eternal, immortal, invisible, the only God, be honour and glory forever and ever. Amen."*
> —1 Timothy 1:17.

Genesis reveals that God saw everything He had made, and it was *"very good"* (**Genesis 1:31**). He placed mankind at the centre of this creation, entrusting them with stewardship over it. Humanity was not an afterthought, but the pinnacle of God's work: created in His image, made to rule, reflect His glory, and enjoy His presence.

God's plan for mankind was deeply intentional and rooted in love. He formed people to bear His image and carry out His purposes on earth. This divine imprint endowed humanity with dignity, responsibility, and the privilege of knowing God. They were to steward creation, not exploit it—mirroring God's care and order.

God also called humanity to fruitfulness and increase: not just to fill the earth, but to multiply His image through generations that honoured Him. To sustain this flourishing life, God provided a perfect home—Eden.

Eden was a paradise of peace, provision, and divine presence. It was not merely a location, but a symbol of what life with God was meant to be: whole, joyful, and eternal. Humanity was given access to the Tree of

Life and the opportunity to live forever in communion with the Creator. This was the heart of God's plan: an eternal relationship filled with love, purpose, and growth.

But something went wrong. Into this perfect and intentional design came a deceiver—crafty, cunning, and calculated in his rebellion against God. Satan, the adversary, entered the garden with a single aim: to disrupt the fellowship between God and humanity, and to twist the truth of God's word. Through deception and doubt, he led Adam and Eve into disobedience, fracturing the harmony of creation and introducing sin into the human story.

Yet, even in this tragic fall, God's plan of love and redemption remained unshaken. In the next chapter, we will expose the tactics and lies of Satan, the great deceiver, and unveil the truth about his role in humanity's fall and God's unwavering response.

CHAPTER

SATAN—THE DECEIVER EXPOSED

> *"He replied, 'I saw Satan fall like lightning from heaven.'"*
> — Luke 10:18

C ontrary to popular belief, Satan is not the opposite of God. He is not equal in power, wisdom, or authority. Satan is a created being —formed by God and subject to Him. While he actively opposes God's purposes, he cannot rival God in any true sense.

God is eternal and sovereign; Satan is finite and defeated. Comparing the two means misunderstanding both. Satan is indeed powerful, but he is still under the supreme authority of the Creator.

Most importantly, Satan's defeat is not hypothetical; it is assured. **Revelation 12:7-9** makes this clear:

> *"And war broke out in heaven: Michael and his angels fought with the dragon... but he was*

> *not strong enough, and they lost their place in heaven. The great dragon was hurled down—that ancient serpent called the devil, or Satan, who leads the whole world astray."*

What is especially striking is that this victory was not executed directly by God, but by Michael the archangel. This further emphasises Satan's inferiority—he was cast out by one of God's created servants.

Over time, culture and folklore have painted Satan as a grotesque, horned creature designed to incite fear. However, Scripture presents a very different picture. Satan is a spiritual being, like the angels. He does not roam around as a physical monster, but often operates subtly through deception. This is why many don't even recognise his influence. He appears not as a demon in rags, but as a counterfeit of good.

> *"And no wonder! For Satan himself masquerades as an angel of light"*
> (2 Corinthians 11:14).

He does not always come with threats—sometimes he comes with enticing promises. But behind the mask, he remains what Jesus called him: *"the father of lies"* (John 8:44).

Some people ask, 'Where did Satan come from?'

While Scripture does not offer an exhaustive biography, it does make his origin clear: he was created by God. **Colossians 1:16** tells us, *"For in Him all things were created: things in heaven and on earth, visible and invisible... all things have been created through Him and for Him."*

Like all created beings, Satan exists under God's authority. He did not originate from darkness; he chose it. The Bible also reveals Satan's fall from grace. **Ezekiel 28:12-17** provides a symbolic but detailed description of a being many scholars associate with Satan: *"You were the seal of perfection, full of wisdom and perfect in beauty... You were anointed as a guardian cherub... You were blameless in your ways from the day you were created till wickedness was found in you."*

His pride, driven by his beauty and wisdom, led to rebellion: *"Your heart became proud on account of your beauty... so I threw you to the earth."* Similarly,

Isaiah 14:12-15 speaks of a heavenly being who sought to usurp God's throne: *"I will ascend above the heights of the clouds; I will be like the Most High."* But God declares: *"You shall be brought down to Sheol, to the lowest depths of the Pit."*

Satan's character is scattered across Scripture, often in roles designed to oppose and harm humanity. As the Great Deceiver, he was present at the very beginning of human history. In **Genesis 3,** he appeared as a serpent, deceiving Eve and leading humanity into sin. That single act introduced death, brokenness, and separation from God.

Jesus later exposed him as a liar by nature:

> *"When he lies, he speaks his native language, for he is a liar and the father of lies."*
> —John 8:44.

He is also the Accuser of the brethren. In **Job 1:6-12,** Satan appears before God to accuse Job of being faithful only because of God's blessings. This same tactic is seen in **Revelation 12:10,** where Satan is described as *"the accuser of our brothers and sisters, who accuses them before our God day and night."*

His goal is to burden believers with guilt, shame, and fear. But we are not left defenceless—Jesus Christ stands as our advocate (**1 John 2:1**).

Satan continues his assault by acting as the Tempter and Thief. He lures people with half-truths, temporary pleasures, and pride. Even Jesus was not exempt—Satan tried to tempt Him in the wilderness with food, fame, and power (**Matthew 4:1-11**). His ultimate goal, as Jesus stated, is *"to steal, kill, and destroy"* (**John 10:10**). He targets the mind with lies, the heart with doubt, and the will with rebellion.

Although Satan is not omnipotent, he wields influence over the fallen systems of the world. Jesus referred to him as *"the ruler of this world"* (**John 12:31**), and Paul described him as *"the god of this age who has blinded the minds of unbelievers"* (**2 Corinthians 4:4**). This influence explains much of the chaos, moral decay, and injustice seen in societies.

Still, Satan's control is temporary and limited. We must never forget that, nor should we forget that his defeat is sealed. He cannot move beyond what God permits (**Job 1:12**). Jesus came *"to destroy the works of the devil"* (**1 John 3:8**), and by His death and resurrection, He disarmed the spiritual powers and triumphed over them (**Colossians 2:15**).

One day, Satan's final judgment will be executed. **Revelation 20:10** declares his end: *"And the devil... was thrown into the lake of burning sulfur... and will be tormented day and night forever and ever."*

Now you may ask, 'Why is Satan so fixated on mankind?'

The answer lies in God's love. Humanity is God's image-bearer (**Genesis 1:27**). Satan hates what God loves and envies the destiny God has prepared for us. From the very beginning, his lies fractured the perfect relationship between God and humanity. The fall of mankind in the Garden of Eden was not just a moral failure—it was the shattering of our identity as God's image-bearers. Yet even in our rebellion, God's pursuit of mankind never ceased.

The next chapter explores the devastating consequences of man's fall, and more importantly, the unwavering love of the Creator who still seeks to restore what was broken. Man may have fallen, but he is not forsaken. God still pursues him with relentless love and a redemptive plan.

CHAPTER

3

MAN—THE FALLEN IMAGE-BEARER, STILL DEEPLY PURSUED

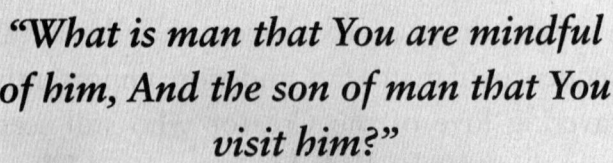

"What is man that You are mindful of him, And the son of man that You visit him?"
—Psalm 8:4

Let us consider the origin of man's creation.

> **Genesis 1:26-27 –** *Then God said, "Let Us make man in Our image, according to Our likeness; let them have dominion over the fish of the sea, over the birds of the air, and over the cattle, over all the earth and over every creeping thing that creeps on the earth."*

So God created man in His own image; in the image of God He created him; male and female He created them.

> **Genesis 2:7 –** *And the LORD God formed man of the dust of the ground, and breathed into his nostrils the breath of life; and man became a living being.*

> **Genesis 2:21-22 – *And the Lord God caused a deep sleep to fall on Adam, and he slept; and He took one of his ribs, and closed up the flesh in its place. Then the rib which the Lord God had taken from man, He made into a woman, and He brought her to the man.***

According to Scripture, man is not the result of random chance or cosmic accident. Humanity is the intentional and precious creation of a loving God. From the very beginning, we see that man was made in the image and likeness of God.

Genesis 1:27 declares,

> ***"So God created man in His own image, in the image of God He created him; male and female He created them."***

This divine imprint, known as the Imago Dei, means that every human being carries intrinsic worth and dignity. We are not like the animals or the rest of creation. We were designed to reflect God's character, think rationally, make moral choices, create beauty, and live in relationships of love and purpose.

Man is both a physical and spiritual being.

Genesis 2:7 tells us that *God formed man from the dust of the earth and then breathed into his nostrils the breath of life, and man became a living being.* This shows that humans are a unique *blend of body and spirit.* The dust speaks of our earthly frame, while God's breath signifies our spiritual identity. We are more than just physical bodies; we are spiritual beings, created to live in communion with the eternal God.

Furthermore, man was created for *relationships.* Our deepest longing to be known, loved, and understood points to the One who made us for Himself. Jesus summed up the greatest commandment in these words: *"You shall love the Lord your God with all your heart and with all your soul and with all your mind"* (**Matthew 22:37**). From the Garden of Eden, where God walked with Adam, to the present day, God's desire has always been for intimate fellowship with His people. We were created not just to exist, but to live in a loving relationship with our Creator and with one another.

Yet, Scripture also reveals that man is a *moral* and *responsible* being. God gave Adam and Eve the ability to choose—to obey or disobey. This capacity for moral choice is a sacred gift, but it also brings accountability. In **Deuteronomy 30:15**, God says, *"See, I have set before you today life and good, death and evil."*

Tragically, the first humans chose to disobey God, and sin entered the world.

Romans 3:23 declares, *"For all have sinned and fall short of the glory of God."* Sin is not merely a bad habit; it is a deep separation from the God who made us. It distorts our identity, damages our relationships, and distances us from our true purpose.

Yet, despite our rebellion, man remains deeply loved by God. **Psalm 8:4** asks, *"What is man that You are mindful of him, and the son of man that You care for him?"* God's care for humanity is not sentimental; it is sacrificial.

In the same way, **Romans 5:8** tells us, *"But God demonstrates His love for us in this: While we were still sinners, Christ died for us."* Even in our fallen state, God saw our value and sent His Son to redeem us. The cross is the clearest evidence of humanity's worth in God's eyes.

Finally, the Bible teaches that man is an eternal being. Our existence does not end with death. **Matthew 25:46** speaks plainly: *"Then they will go away to eternal punishment, but the righteous to eternal life."* We were made for eternity, and every soul will spend forever either in the presence of God or separated from Him. This reality gives weight to every decision we make in this life. **Hebrews 9:27** reminds us, *"It is appointed for man to die once, and after that comes judgment."*

In summary, man is a divinely crafted, spiritually endowed, morally accountable, deeply loved, and eternally destined being. We were made for more than survival. We were made for glory, for relationship, for purpose, and for God. Yet sin has marred the image we bear, and without divine intervention, we are lost. This is why the rescue plan matters. It is not just about fixing what is broken but about restoring humanity to its original design: walking in fellowship with God and bearing His likeness once again.

Once we understand who man is—a being made in God's image but corrupted by sin—it becomes clear why humanity needs saving. We are not merely victims of our environment or products of broken systems. At our core, we are spiritually broken and separated from God. Sin is not just a list of wrong actions; it is a condition of the heart, a deep-rooted rebellion against our Creator.

As **Romans 3:23** states, *"All have sinned and fall short of the glory of God."* This falling short is not a minor flaw—it is a complete disconnection from the life and holiness of God.

In the Garden of Eden, when Adam and Eve disobeyed God, they not only broke His command—but they broke the relationship. Sin entered the world, and with it came guilt, shame, fear, and death.

Romans 5:12 says,

> *"Just as sin entered the world through one man, and death through sin, in this way death came to all people, because all sinned."*

From that moment on, every person born into this world inherited a sinful nature. It affects our thoughts, our choices, our relationships, and ultimately our destiny.

Because God is holy, He cannot ignore sin. His justice demands a response. Yet, because God is also love, He made a way for justice and mercy to meet. The law of God reveals His perfect standards, but it also shows us how far we have fallen. No amount of good deeds or moral effort can erase the stain of sin.

As **Isaiah 64:6** declares, ***"All our righteous acts are like filthy rags."*** This means we cannot save ourselves. We need someone pure, perfect, and powerful enough to rescue us from sin's penalty and restore us to God.

This is why man needs a Saviour—not merely a teacher, not just a prophet, and not a religious system. We need someone who can do what we cannot: bridge the gap between a holy God and sinful man. We need a Saviour who is both fully God and fully man, someone who can represent us before God and satisfy the demands of divine justice. That Saviour is Jesus Christ.

CHAPTER

JESUS—THE PERFECT, DIVINE RESCUER

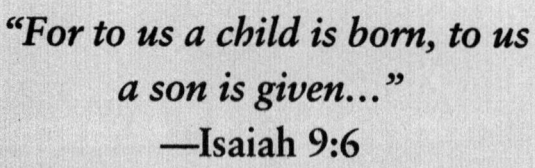

"For to us a child is born, to us a son is given..."
—Isaiah 9:6

To understand what Jesus did for us, we must first recognise who He is.

Long before Jesus was born in Bethlehem, His coming was foretold. The promise of a Saviour echoes from the very beginning of Scripture, woven through the Old Testament like a golden thread pointing to one hope: God would send a Redeemer.

The first whisper of this promise came in the Garden of Eden. After Adam and Eve sinned, God did not leave them in despair. Instead, He declared war on the serpent and spoke a prophetic word in **Genesis 3:15**:

> *"And I will put enmity between you and the woman, and between your offspring and hers; He will crush your head, and you will strike His heel."*

This is known as the Protoevangelium—the first gospel. It pointed to a future descendant of the woman who would defeat Satan and undo the curse of sin. That descendant is Jesus Christ.

As history unfolded, God continued to speak through prophets, priests, and kings. Each one pointing to the coming Messiah. The prophet Isaiah, writing over 700 years before Christ's birth, declared:

> *"Therefore the Lord Himself will give you a sign: The virgin will conceive and give birth to a son, and will call Him Immanuel"*
> —Isaiah 7:14.

And again in Isaiah 9:6:

> *"For to us a child is born, to us a son is given, and the government will be on His shoulders. And He will be called Wonderful Counsellor, Mighty God, Everlasting Father, Prince of Peace."*

Micah the prophet even named the town where the Messiah would be born:

> *"But you, Bethlehem Ephrathah, though you are small among the clans of Judah, out of you will come for Me one who will be ruler over Israel, whose origins are from of old, from ancient times." —Micah 5:2.*

Throughout the Old Testament, Christ is concealed in types and shadows. He is the true Ark of Noah, saving humanity from judgment. He is the promised seed of Abraham, through whom all nations would be blessed (**Genesis 22:18**). He is the Passover Lamb in Exodus, whose blood protects from death. He is the bronze serpent lifted in the wilderness, healing those who look upon Him. He is foreshadowed in every sacrifice, every priestly intercession, and every promise of deliverance.

The Psalms sing of Him. David writes, *"They pierced my hands and my feet"* (Psalm 22:16) and *"The Lord said to my Lord: 'Sit at My right hand until I make Your enemies a footstool for Your feet'"* (Psalm 110:1).

The prophets envisioned His mission with startling clarity. **Isaiah 53** speaks of a Suffering Servant who would bear the sins of many:

> *"He was pierced for our transgressions, He was crushed for our iniquities... and by His wounds we are healed."*

Then, in the fullness of time, the promise became flesh. The angel Gabriel appeared to a virgin named Mary and said:

> *"You will conceive and give birth to a son, and you are to call Him Jesus. He will be great and will be called the Son of the Most High"* —Luke 1:31-32.

Jesus was born of a virgin, conceived by the Holy Spirit—fully God and fully man. He entered our world not with royalty, but with humility: a baby born in a manger. Yet heaven rejoiced. The angels sang to shepherds in the fields,

> *"A Saviour has been born to you; He is the Messiah, the Lord"* —Luke 2:11.

As He grew, Jesus fulfilled every prophecy. He was baptised by John, tempted in the wilderness, and proclaimed the kingdom of God. He healed the sick, raised the dead, fed the multitudes, and spoke with divine authority. He was no ordinary teacher. He forgave sins, calmed storms, and cast out demons—acts only God can do. He fulfilled the law completely and walked in perfect obedience.

But His mission was not simply to perform miracles or preach the truth. Jesus came to save us from our sins. As John the Baptist declared, *"Behold, the Lamb of God, who takes away the sin of the world!"* (John 1:29). The cross was not an interruption to His mission; it was the very purpose of it. Jesus Himself said,

> *"The Son of Man came not to be served but to serve, and to give His life as a ransom for many"* (Mark 10:45).

He was betrayed, arrested, falsely accused, beaten, and nailed to a cross. Yet He willingly endured it all. Why? Because He loves us. Because only His blood could pay the price for our redemption. On the cross, the righteous One became sin for us, so that we might become the righteousness of God (2 Corinthians 5:21).

Just as foretold, He did not stay dead. On the third day, He rose again. His resurrection was the ultimate victory—not only over death, but over sin, shame, and Satan. The grave could not hold Him. He appeared to His disciples, commissioned them to spread the good news, and ascended into heaven, where He now reigns as King and Intercessor.

From Genesis to Revelation, the Bible tells one grand story: the story of Jesus. He is the promised seed, the coming King, the suffering Servant, the risen Lord, and the returning Judge. Every page whispers His name. Every prophecy finds its *"Yes"* in Him.

Jesus didn't come to improve our lives; He came to save our souls. His mission was not to fix the surface but to transform our hearts. He came to restore what was lost, heal what was broken, and bring us back to the Father. Through Him, the rescue plan of God is complete.

Jesus is not merely a religious figure or moral teacher; He is the eternal Son of God, the Word made flesh, fully God and fully man. **John 1:14** tells us, ***"The Word became flesh and dwelt among us."*** He left the glory of heaven and entered our broken world, not to observe it, but to redeem it from within. His mission was clear from the start:

> *"The Son of Man came to seek and to save the lost"* (Luke 19:10).

Jesus lived a life of perfect obedience to the Father. Where humanity failed repeatedly, Jesus stood firm. Every word He spoke and every action He took were in complete alignment with God's will. **Hebrews 4:15** says, *"He was tempted in every way, just as we are—yet was without sin."* This sinless life was essential, for only a spotless sacrifice could pay the price for sin. Jesus fulfilled the law in every detail, offering a righteousness that we could never achieve on our own.

At the cross, Jesus became our substitute. This is the core of the gospel—substitutionary atonement.

Isaiah 53:6 declares, *"The Lord has laid on Him the iniquity of us all."* Though He was innocent, He bore our guilt. Though He knew no sin, He became sin for us (**2 Corinthians 5:21**). The nails in His hands were meant for us. The judgment he faced was ours to bear.

He suffered not just physically, but spiritually —enduring separation from the Father so we could be brought near.

On the cross, He cried, *"My God, my God, why have You forsaken Me?"* (Matthew 27:46). In that moment, the weight of every sin—past, present, and future—rested upon Him. He drank the full cup of God's wrath so that we could drink the cup of His grace.

Jesus truly died. His body was taken down from the cross, wrapped in linen, and laid in a tomb. This was no illusion, no symbolic act. His death was real and necessary, for *"without the shedding of blood there is no forgiveness of sins"* (Hebrews 9:22). He entered the silence of death so that He could conquer it from the inside out.

On the third day, Jesus did what no one else in history has done—He rose from the dead by His power. The resurrection is the foundation of our hope. As Paul boldly declared, *"If Christ has not been raised, your faith is futile; you are still in your sins"* (1 Corinthians 15:17). But Christ has been raised, and because of that, sin has been defeated, the grave has lost its sting, and eternal life has been secured for all who believe.

Jesus' resurrection proves His divinity, confirms His victory, and guarantees ours. It was not only the vindication of His identity, but the validation of His mission. Through the resurrection, He broke the power of death and opened the door to eternal life.

Acts 1:9-11 tells us:

> *"Now when He had spoken these things, while they watched, He was taken up, and a cloud received Him out of their sight. And while they looked steadfastly toward heaven as He went up, behold, two men stood by them in white apparel, who also said, "Men of Galilee, why do you stand gazing up into heaven? This same Jesus, who was taken up from you into heaven, will come in like manner as you saw Him go into heaven."*

Jesus did not return to the tomb; He ascended to heaven, where He is now seated at the right hand of God. From there, He reigns with all authority and power. He is not distant or detached.

Romans 8:34 says,

> *"Christ Jesus who died—more than that, who was raised to life—is at the right hand of God and is also interceding for us."*

Right now, Jesus is praying for His people, standing as our great High Priest, and preparing a place for us in eternity.

The story is not finished. The same Jesus who came in humility will return in glory. **Revelation 1:7** says,

> *"Behold, He is coming with the clouds, and every eye will see Him."*

He will return as King and Judge to fully establish His kingdom, to wipe away every tear, and to make all things new.

When Jesus ascended to heaven, He did not leave us unprotected or alone. Instead, He sent us a divine Helper—the Holy Spirit, also known as the Comforter—to be our ever-present guide and guard.

CHAPTER

THE HOLY SPIRIT—OUR SEAL, OUR STRENGTH, OUR GUIDE

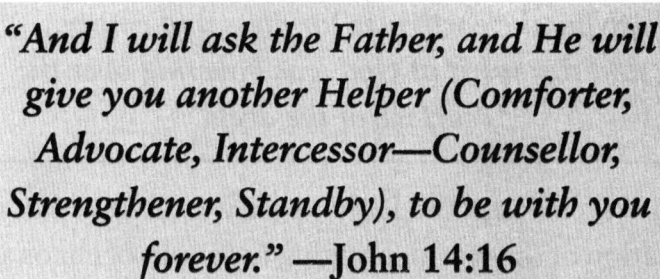

"And I will ask the Father, and He will give you another Helper (Comforter, Advocate, Intercessor—Counsellor, Strengthener, Standby), to be with you forever." —John 14:16

The Holy Spirit is not merely a force, symbol, or influence; He is God. He is the third Person of the Trinity, co-equal and co-eternal with the Father and the Son. From the opening verses of Genesis to the closing words of Revelation, the Holy Spirit is present, active, and essential to God's redemptive plan.

In **Genesis 1:2,** the Spirit is introduced as the breath of God, hovering over the waters:

> *"Now the earth was formless and empty...*
> *and the Spirit of God was hovering over the*
> *surface of the deep."*

This reveals that the Holy Spirit was involved in the creation of the world, bringing order out of chaos and light out of darkness. Throughout the Old Testament, the Holy Spirit came upon individuals to empower them for specific divine tasks. In **Exodus 31:1-5**, we read:

> *"Then the Lord spoke to Moses, saying:*
> *"See, I have called by name Bezalel the son*
> *of Uri, the son of Hur, of the tribe of Judah.*
> *And I have filled him with the Spirit of God,*
> *in wisdom, in understanding, in knowledge,*
> *and in all manner of workmanship, to*
> *design artistic works, to work in gold, in*
> *silver, in bronze, in cutting jewels for*
> *setting, in carving wood, and to work in all*
> *manner of workmanship."*

Here, the Holy Spirit empowered Bezalel with the skill and wisdom needed to construct the tabernacle.

In **Judges 14:5-6**, we see another example:

> *"So Samson went down to Timnah with his*
> *father and mother, and came to the*
> *vineyards of Timnah. Now, to his surprise, a*
> *young lion came roaring against him. And*
> *the Spirit of the Lord came mightily upon*
> *him, and he tore the lion apart as one would*

> *have torn apart a young goat, though he had nothing in his hand. But he did not tell his father or his mother what he had done."*

The Holy Spirit gave Samson supernatural strength. David was anointed king (**1 Samuel 16:13**), and the prophets were inspired to proclaim God's messages (**2 Peter 1:21**).

However, during this era, the Spirit's presence was temporary and selective. He did not dwell permanently within individuals. These instances were prophetic shadows, pointing forward to a time when the Spirit would be poured out on all of God's people. This God-given promise was clearly articulated through the prophets. Joel prophesied:

> *"And afterwards, I will pour out My Spirit on all people. Your sons and daughters will prophesy..."* —Joel 2:28.

Ezekiel declared:

"I will put My Spirit in you and move you to follow My decrees" —**Ezekiel 36:27**. These promises anticipated a future era in which the Holy Spirit

would not merely come upon believers, but would dwell within them. Before His crucifixion, Jesus reassured His disciples that the Holy Spirit would come. In **John 14:16-17**, He said:

> *"I will ask the Father, and He will give you another Helper, to be with you forever—the Spirit of truth... He lives with you and will be in you."*

The Greek word used here, Parakletos, can be translated as helper, comforter, advocate, or counsellor. The Holy Spirit would not only dwell with believers but also guide, comfort, and empower them to live out their faith. This promise was fulfilled on the day of Pentecost. **In Acts 2:2-4,** as the early believers waited in prayer, *"Suddenly a sound like the blowing of a violent wind came from heaven... They saw what seemed to be tongues of fire... All of them were filled with the Holy Spirit."*

This historic moment marked the birth of the Church and the beginning of the new covenant era, in which the Spirit was given not just to a few but to all who believe in Jesus Christ. One of the most profound roles of the Holy Spirit is to seal believers for salvation. Paul writes:

> *"When you believed, you were marked in Him with a seal, the promised Holy Spirit, who is a deposit guaranteeing our inheritance"*
> —Ephesians 1:13-14.

In ancient times, a seal symbolised ownership, authenticity, and security. In the same way, the Holy Spirit seals believers, marking them as God's own and assuring them of the eternal inheritance promised through Christ. The Holy Spirit is also our source of strength. The Christian life can not be lived through human effort alone. Jesus said:

> *"You will receive power when the Holy Spirit comes on you"*
> —Acts 1:8.

This power (dynamis in Greek) gives believers the ability to overcome sin, resist temptation, endure suffering, and boldly proclaim the gospel. Paul prayed that believers would be *"strengthened with power through His Spirit in your inner being"* (Ephesians 3:16). It is by the strength of the Spirit that we bear fruit and grow into spiritual maturity.

Beyond sealing and empowering, the Holy Spirit is also our guide. Jesus said in **John 16:13,** *"But when He, the Spirit of truth, comes, He will guide you into all truth... He will glorify Me."* The Spirit teaches, reminds, convicts, and leads us. He helps us understand Scripture (**1 Corinthians 2:12-14**), aligns our decisions with God's will (**Romans 8:14**), and intercedes for us in prayer when words fail (**Romans 8:26**). His guidance is personal, gentle, and always in harmony with God's Word.

The presence of the Holy Spirit results in transformation. Paul calls this the fruit of the Spirit in **Galatians 5:22-23:**

> *"Love, joy, peace, forbearance, kindness, goodness, faithfulness, gentleness, and self-control."*

These qualities are not the product of human effort but of the Spirit's work within us. They demonstrate that God is actively shaping us into the image of Christ. The Holy Spirit is not distant; He is God's presence within you. He convicts of sin, assures you of your salvation, fills you with purpose, and equips you to live for Christ. If you belong to Jesus, the Holy

Spirit dwells within you—you are never alone. Allow Him to lead you. Yield to His work, and He will continue to transform you, strengthen you, and seal you until the day of Christ's return.

Paul writes:

> *"In Him you also trusted, after you heard the word of truth, the gospel of your salvation; in whom also, having believed, you were sealed with the Holy Spirit of promise, who is the guarantee of our inheritance until the redemption of the purchased possession, to the praise of His glory."*
> —Ephesians 1:16-17.

One may ask: how do I know all these things are true and not mere fabricated tales?

CHAPTER

THE BIBLE—THE TRUSTWORTHY, LIVING ROADMAP OF GOD'S TRUTH

"All Scripture is given by inspiration of God, and is profitable for doctrine, for reproof, for correction, for instruction in righteousness, that the man of God may be complete, thoroughly equipped for every good work."
—2 Timothy 3:16

The Bible is a remarkable collection of 66 books, written by over 40 different human authors across approximately 1,500 years and three continents: Asia, Africa, and Europe. Despite the diversity of its authors—which included kings, prophets, fishermen, shepherds, military leaders, and scholars—the message of the Bible remains unified and consistent. It reveals God's nature, His covenant with humanity, and His plan of redemption through Jesus Christ.

The Bible is divided into two main sections: the Old Testament, comprising 39 books, and the New Testament, containing 27 books. These authors were inspired by the Holy Spirit (**2 Timothy 3:16; 2 Peter 1:21**), ensuring that the Scripture is not a product of human imagination but the very breath of God communicated through human vessels.

Originally, the books of the Bible were not written with chapter and verse divisions. The texts appeared as scrolls, letters, or historical narratives without numbered sections. The chapter divisions we use today were introduced much later for ease of reading and reference. Chapters were added around the 13th century by *Stephen Langton, the Archbishop of Canterbury*, while verses were introduced in the 16th century by scholars such as *Robert Estienne*. Although these divisions are helpful tools for study, teaching, and memorisation, they serve primarily to allow readers across the world to locate and reflect on God's Word with shared clarity and structure.

Throughout history, efforts have been made both to challenge and to confirm the truth of the gospel of Christ. Scholars, historians, theologians, and sceptics have all examined the claims of Christianity. From this vast landscape of inquiry, two major categories of evidence have emerged: *internal evidence* and *external evidence.*

External Evidence involves tangible historical and archaeological elements that support the reliability of the events described in the Christian faith. These include ancient structures, city ruins, political figures, and documented historical events that align with the Bible's timeline. When examined, many of these elements correspond to the political and cultural context of the times described in Scripture, affirming that the biblical narrative is grounded in real history rather than merely mythical storytelling.

For instance, Luke opens his Gospel by carefully situating the birth of Jesus within a specific historical and political context: *"In those days Caesar Augustus issued a decree that a census should be taken..."* (**Luke 2:1**). Similarly, the names of rulers such as Herod, Pilate, and Festus, and places such as Nazareth, Jerusalem, and Caesarea, are all verified by historical and archaeological records.

On the other hand, **Internal Evidence** draws from the integrity of the documents themselves and the testimony of those who wrote and experienced the events firsthand. The message of the gospel was not passed down as folklore or hearsay; it was delivered by people who witnessed the life, death, and resurrection of Jesus directly. The Apostle Paul wrote:

> *"I delivered to you as of first importance what I also received: that Christ died for our*

> *sins according to the Scriptures, that He was buried, that He was raised on the third day... and that He appeared to Cephas, then to the twelve. After that, He appeared to more than five hundred brothers at once... then He appeared to James, then to all the apostles; and last of all... to me also"*
> (1 Corinthians 15:3-8).

These eyewitnesses were not only testifying to what they saw, but they were willing to die for it. The transformation of men like Peter—who once denied Jesus out of fear (**Luke 22:61-62**)—into bold preachers of the resurrection (**Acts 2:32**) is compelling. Peter himself declared, *"God has raised this Jesus to life, and we are all witnesses of it"* (Acts 2:32).

In another epistle, he emphasised:

> *"We did not follow cleverly devised stories when we told you about the coming of our Lord Jesus Christ in power, but we were eyewitnesses of His majesty"*
> (2 Peter 1:16).

What is even more striking is that these eyewitnesses pointed to a surer and more enduring evidence—the Scriptures. After describing the moment he heard the voice of God affirm Jesus on the Mount of Transfiguration, Peter said, *"We also have the prophetic word confirmed, which you do well to heed as a light that shines in a dark place..."* (2 Peter 1:19). He explained further that, *"No prophecy of Scripture comes from one's own interpretation, for prophecy never came by the will of man, but holy men of God spoke as they were moved by the Holy Spirit"* (2 Peter 1:20-21).

This points us to the authority and consistency of Scripture. The Bible is not merely a religious document; it is a cohesive, prophetic revelation. Paul reinforces this when he writes, *"All Scripture is God-breathed and is useful for teaching, rebuking, correcting and training in righteousness"* (2 Timothy 3:16). For the early church, the written Word was not just a support for their testimony; it was the foundation upon which their entire faith was built.

This highlights the extraordinary nature of the Christian faith: it is rooted not only in personal experience but also in historical fulfilment and divine revelation. The Scriptures serve as both a prophetic and interpretive lens through which the life and work of Jesus are understood. They bring coherence to the gospel story, showing that what happened in the past was always part of God's divine rescue plan. From the promise to Abraham in **Genesis 12:3,** to the Suffering Servant in **Isaiah 53,** to the New Covenant foretold in **Jeremiah 31,** the Old Testament anticipated the Messiah—and in Jesus, that promise was fulfilled (**Luke 24:27**).

The Scriptures form the trustworthy, living roadmap of God's truth. They are reliable not only because they align with historical and archaeological findings but because they reveal a consistent message of redemption, foretold by the prophets, fulfilled in Christ, and confirmed by His followers. From Genesis to Revelation, the Bible unfolds a divine narrative that reveals the heart, plan, and purpose of God.

In a world full of changing opinions, moral ambiguity, and spiritual confusion, the Bible remains a steady compass. It serves as a guide to our past as well as our future. Its truth does not shift with time, and its authority is not diminished by doubt. Instead, it invites each generation to discover and trust the eternal God who speaks through its pages.

Conclusion

The gospel is not merely a message to be received; it is a message to be believed, a truth to be lived, and a relationship to be embraced. From the beginning, God's heart has been to dwell with His people, to love them, restore them, and draw them into a life of wholeness and purpose. Despite sin's distortion, God's plan remained intact. Through Jesus Christ, God made a way for everything to be made new.

Each chapter of this book has offered a glimpse into that divine rescue plan, revealing a God who creates with intention, a deceiver who distorts, a humanity that fell but is still pursued, a Saviour who redeems, a Spirit who empowers, and a Word that guides. The gospel answers our deepest questions and meets our greatest needs. It is more than religion; it is redemption. It is more than a story; it is salvation.

The invitation is simple yet life-changing: believe in the Lord Jesus and be saved. Walk with the one true God whose redeeming arms are wide open. The Scripture says that God is not slow concerning His promise, as some understand slowness. Instead, He is patient with you, not wanting anyone to perish but everyone to come to repentance. Step into the rescue plan that was written with you in mind from the very beginning.